20 LESSONS THAT BUILD A MAN'S FINANCES

20 LESSONS THAT BUILD A MAN'S FINANCES

A CONVERSATIONAL MENTORING GUIDE

VINCE MILLER

EQUIP PRESS

Colorado Springs

Published by Equip Press, Colorado Springs, CO

First Edition: 2020
20 Lessons That Build A Man's Finances / Vince Miller
Paperback ISBN: 978-1-951304-19-5
eBook ISBN: 978-1-951304-20-1

TO: ______________________________

FROM: ______________________________

NOTE: ______________________________

CONTENTS

A NOTE FROM THE AUTHOR

Leading your finances seems impossible. Some days you will make great financial decisions, and other days not so much. This is because managing, making, and spending money reveals the story of a man's desires. Many of the lessons you will discover in this book were passed on to me by others who are far more successful than me in this area, and the others were learned from my greatest mentor–failure.

My hope for you is that these lessons give you something to discuss with a friend, relative, coworker, or even your children. I hope they will stir a discussion that will give you an opportunity to proactively pass on wisdom. May this mentoring relationship lead to greater success as you lead your business, team, non-profit, church, or your very own family.

Join in a mentorship movement and mentor or be mentored.

Keep moving forward,

Live all in,

USING 20 LESSONS THAT BUILD A MAN'S FINANCES

The Purpose

This twenty-lesson guide is for mentors to use in private reflection or conversations with others. It's written to invite leadership and character development conversations for people of any age and can be used repeatedly.

The Process

First, build yourself

Read through one lesson each time and ponder privately on the reflection questions within the lesson. Each lesson uses the B.U.I.L.D. process.

- BEGIN with the goal.
- UNPACK your thoughts.
- INFORM through the Bible.
- LAND on action steps.
- DO one action for one week.

Second, partner up

Take each lesson further by partnering up with someone else. Use the twenty lessons as a mentoring tool that takes all the guesswork out of a leadership development conversation. Partner up with a friend, relative, co-worker, or someone in your family.

The Payoff

If you stay with the process for all twenty lessons, you will grow in character, in your leadership, and in community with others. Often, we just need a plan to get moving. This book provides that plan—a method and a process that results in outcomes with a rich payoff.

SPEAKER & AUTHOR VINCE MILLER

Abandoned by his drug-using father at the age of two, Vince Miller grew up in a challenging and anxiety-producing environment. He endured the strain of his mother's two failed marriages as well as her poor choices and drug use. Fortunately, during Vince's formative teen years, his grandfather, a man of faith, stepped up to mentor Vince, guiding him through a particularly difficult period.

Though he resisted initially, Vince became a follower of Christ at the age of twenty. Soon after, he would be with his grandfather on his deathbed as cancer took his life. At that time, Vince committed before God to give back by mentoring men as his grandfather had mentored him. Vince's story demonstrates the importance of mentors to support others in overcoming the enormous hurdles that manhood, mentoring, fathering, and leadership present to a man who wants to live in faith and character.

Audiences respond to Vince's stories and teaching that motivate, convict, and sometimes even shock. He inspires men to lead and mentor others with an intelligent argument for faith and stories of choices he made as a man, husband, father, and leader.

After serving in notable organizations for over twenty-six years (including Young Life, InterVarsity, and TCU Football), Vince founded Resolute, a non-profit organization focused on providing men with tools for mentorship. He's written seventeen books and Bible study handbooks, along with creating small group videos that are resources for mentorship.

He also produces a daily writing known as *The Men's Daily Devotional* read by thousands daily.

If you are looking for a motivational and engaging communicator for your next retreat, conference, or event, reach out to Vince Miller directly through his website at www.vincemiller.com.

Provider of Provision

And Isaac said to his father Abraham, "My father!" And he said, "Here I am, my son." He said, "Behold, the fire and the wood, but where is the lamb for a burnt offering?" Abraham said, "God will provide for himself the lamb for a burnt offering, my son." So they went both of them together.

GENESIS 22:7-8

It is not the strength of your faith but the object of your faith that actually saves you.

TIMOTHY KELLER

Many men of the Old Testament were remarkable leaders, pioneers, and patriarchs in our early faith. One of these men was Abraham. He is known by many as the "father of faith." And he bears this title because he was willing to adventure into the great unknown, taking one step at a time with God regardless of the human and natural consequences. When God invited Abraham to depart his hometown of Ur to go to a land he had never seen, he simply trusted God and launched out into the great venture of his life. He had no road map or awareness of the obstacles he would encounter along the way, but he understood that if God asked something of him that He would also provide for him. And God did, time after time.

Thus, it was no different when God told him to adventure into the unthinkable–a human sacrifice of his only son Isaac on the Mountain of the Lord. Yet, strangely enough, Abraham did the unthinkable; he quickly obeyed. He took his son and the wood they needed and climbed the mountain immediately. Isaac's inquiry on the way up the mountain still startles mothers and fathers today:

> *And Isaac said to his father Abraham, "My father!" And he said, "Here I am, my son." He said, "Behold, the fire and the wood, but where is the lamb for a burnt offering?" Abraham said, "God will provide for himself the lamb for a burnt offering, my son." So they went both of them together.*
>
> Genesis 22:7-8

God Is the Provider—Not Us

Abraham walked into a teachable moment that men need to learn. God is the original and only Provider. God is the one who provides for the needs of all mankind. He owns all things. He knows all things. He sees the future of all things. So he provides exactly what we need to be given and when, since he owns, knows, and sees all things from beginning to end. He can provide all that we need at the given moment we need it, which is why Jesus instructs us to pray, "Give us this day our daily bread." It is through a daily and regular provision that God keeps us reliant on Him and from becoming reliant on self. The prophet Jeremiah says it like this:

> *"Blessed is the man who trusts in the Lord, whose trust is the Lord. He is like a tree planted by water, that sends out its roots by the stream, and does not fear when heat comes, for its leaves remain green, and is not anxious in the year of drought, for it does not cease to bear fruit."*
>
> Jeremiah 17:7-8

Every man has needs. The question is whether we look to ourselves as the source of those needs or trust God for them. Wise men understand that it is God who provides. But often we believe we, "the man, the leader, the husband, the father" are the provider. Are we called to be responsible? Yes. Are we called to act like men? Yes. Are we the original provider? No.

Self-reliant men do not stand for long before the Lord, and Abraham was the father of faith because he understood there was one who provided, and he, Abraham, was not it. Yet Abraham was a virtuous, strong, wealthy man of God who understood this one thing; God is the source of all things. He is Lord of my life; therefore, I must quickly obey.

Here are three things a great man remembers.

One | God provides to faithful men.

I the Lord search the heart and test the mind, to give every man according to his ways, according to the fruit of his deeds.

Jeremiah 17:10

God loves to provide. It's His great joy. And God is generous in the way He provides–love, grace, mercy, and forgiveness come in endless quantities because His supply is unlimited. However, in light of this, our response should be the free sharing of His riches with the world. But often, we selfishly withhold these resources. And God never entrusts a man who withholds his free and generous resources. Instead, He seeks men who can steward them appropriately, and He searches their hearts, even tests them along the path of life, and gives according to their ability. While God loves us regardless of our conduct, He provides to those who conduct themselves rightly–these are His faithful men.

Two | God provides what brings Him glory.

My grace is sufficient for you, for my power is made perfect in weakness.

2 Corinthians 12:9

Man exists to bring glory to God. As a result, God provides for us in ways that give us more opportunity to draw attention to His glory. This may well mean that He will choose to provide for our needs in ways we don't expect. The Apostle Paul lived with a deficiency that he asked God to remove. God declined because He wanted Paul and those around him to know that God's "grace is sufficient for you, for my power is made perfect in weakness." Paul responded, "Therefore I will boast all the more gladly of my weaknesses, so that the power of Christ may rest upon me." - 2 Corinthians 12:9.

As God's man, Paul understood that God's strength came not from his power but the Father in, through, and by his weakness. This is counterintuitive for most men, but Paul accepted God's decline because he knew that God provides what brings Him glory. And God is not looking for self-reliant men who want to bring glory to themselves. Instead, God is seeking God-reliant men in whom our weaknesses bring attention to God's ever-expanding glory. This is a hard-learned lesson for many men because we misunderstand the grit and gumption that God seeks.

Three | God is the provider, and the means of provision, man must trust.

God will provide for himself the lamb for a burnt offering, my son.

Genesis 22:8

Whatever needs you may have, God is the source of satisfaction for those needs and the means of meeting those needs. We as men need to invest our whole life in trusting Him to do this perpetually. And for many men, this is challenging, humbling, and often does not work the way we want. Yet we must learn to pray for His provision, and trust He is listening. We must learn to wait for His response and trust His timing. We must learn to not play the follower and let him provide to bring glory to His name and not ours. God is the only reliable provider we have, and as we do this, those around us learn the character of a God who provides for us and can provide for their needs as well. As Abraham said, walking up a mountain where human sacrifice plagued his mind, "God will provide for himself."

We live in an uncertain world. Our source of income could end tomorrow. Our investments could take a catastrophic dive. Our health could change in an instant. While life looks secure today, tomorrow might be different. Whether secure or insecure, we have a God who provides. Whatever your need, trust Him, and He will be faithful to you.

Reflection & Mentorship

Begin

- God is the source for all things we ever need.

Unpack

- Why is it important for man to provide? List some reasons.
- What are the limits of this provision for a Christian man?
- How does your need for provision keep you from making godly decisions like Abraham did with Isaac?

Inform

- The statement, "Behold, the fire and the wood, but where is the lamb for a burnt offering?" is an honest question from an interested son. If you are a father, share what you might be thinking and want to say to your son in this moment.

- Abraham's response is short and to the point, "God will provide for himself the lamb for a burnt offering, my son." What do you think he was thinking based on what he said?

Land

- What issues challenge you when it comes to God being a provider in situations you cannot provide?
- What steps do you need to take to address these challenges?

Do

- Ask God to provide for you where you cannot and wait one week for His provision.

Made to Work

Slaves, obey in everything those who are your earthly masters, not by way of eye-service, as people-pleasers, but with sincerity of heart, fearing the Lord. Whatever you do, work heartily, as for the Lord and not for men, knowing that from the Lord you will receive the inheritance as your reward. You are serving the Lord Christ.

COLOSSIANS 3:22-24

Too many people spend money they earned... to buy things they don't want... to impress people that they don't like.

WILL ROGERS

Do you like your job? Do you hate it? Is work your life, or do you consider it a necessary evil? Maybe you'd rather not have to work at all. Or maybe you've lost your job and would give anything to be hired somewhere, anywhere, just so you can earn an income again.

It's not my intention here to identify all our good and bad attitudes about work and offer pointers to somehow adjust them. Instead, let's explore a biblical perspective about work—with the hope that God will nurture in us the healthiest possible approach to our earthly occupations.

Let's start by stating the obvious. Jesus worked. He was a carpenter. He learned a skill, and He made a living doing it. We will do well to keep that in mind as we consider four key facts about work.

One | We are designed to work.

"The Lord God took the man and put him in the Garden of Eden to work it and keep it."

Genesis 2:15

This was stated before man ever sinned–work is not a consequence of sin. God assigned Adam the task of "working" the Garden of Eden, developing it, making it productive. And he was to "keep" the Garden, to maintain it, to preserve its beauty. He was a gardener, the world's first farmer, employed by the Creator Himself.

Two | We are employed by God.

"Whatever you do, work heartily, as for the Lord and not for men, knowing that from the Lord you will receive the inheritance as your reward. You are serving the Lord Christ."

Colossians 3:23-24

"Whatever you do," says the Bible, whether it be plumbing, accounting, construction, teaching–pick a job, any job (as long as it doesn't violate God's Word, of course)–and work hard at it. We don't have to be employed in some sort of ministerial role in order to be working for God. We are "serving the Lord Christ" regardless of the nature of our labor. So work hard and do your best at whatever you do–it's all for the Lord.

Three | We work to support ourselves and our families.

"For even when we were with you, we would give you this command: If anyone is not willing to work, let him not eat."

2 Thessalonians 3:10

Work is an essential part of life. It's how we feed, clothe, and house ourselves and our families. We earn an income not only so our own needs are met but also so we can generously give to others in need. And notice this phrase: "willing to work." Are you laid off, between jobs, or otherwise unemployed? Well, take heart. Finding a job is work. It requires a full-time effort. So don't give up. Just remember to seek the Lord as you seek employment. Ask for His guidance as you move ahead with your search, and He will give you direction. And be patient. He knows what's ahead. His timing is perfect.

Four | We follow God's example to work at a healthy pace.

"Thus the heavens and the earth were finished, and the host of them. And on the seventh day God finished His work that He had done, and He rested on the seventh day from all His work that He had done."

Genesis 2:1-2

Think about it. Even God worked. He created the universe. But then He rested. He took a break. Carrying their work ethic to an extreme, some guys become "workaholics." The world may find this admirable, but it's certainly not biblical. We must be intentional about achieving a work/life balance–seeking God's wisdom to build in the kind of margin that lets us recoup, recharge, and nurture our relationships with Him and with our friends and families.

I admit it's a plus if you enjoy your work. Some guys do find their niche in a career they love. But keep in mind that our aim is to "work heartily as for the Lord" no matter what we're doing. God often assigns us to tasks that are not particularly "fun." So let our joy come from knowing that we're working for Him, and that our ultimate reward is in our inheritance from Him. After all, a mansion in paradise forever with our Heavenly Father is a pretty good place to end up, don't you think?

Reflection & Mentorship

Begin

- Men must work, as God created us to do good works.

Unpack

- What do you think most men believe about work?
- What evidence can you point to that supports these beliefs?

Inform

Slaves, obey in everything those who are your earthly masters, not by way of eye-service, as people-pleasers, but with sincerity of heart, fearing the Lord. Whatever you do, work heartily, as for the Lord and not for men, knowing that from the Lord you will receive the inheritance as your reward. You are serving the Lord Christ.

Colossians 3:22-24

- Paul is instructing slaves in this situation. In some ways, this was a means of gainful employment in the Roman empire. What is his instruction to them?
- Do you see your work situation in the same light?
- Of the four points above, which one is easy, and which one is hard for you? Why?

Land

- What do you need to do differently?

Do

- Pray for five minutes this week about your beliefs, attitudes, or actions.

Trust God in Fear

Recently a friend told me about a friend of his who sold his business for eighty million dollars equally divided between a mother and a son. The mother decided to immediately make a several-million-dollar gift to ministries she was close to. Her son told her she was foolish to make the gift, as she might need the funds in the future.

This true story illustrates that fearing we won't have enough is not a matter of what we actually have but a fear that is common to those who have little and those who have much. In fact, the more one has, the more one believes they need to have in order to have enough. This is one case where the goalposts do move.

How do we deal with our fear that we won't have enough?

> *Therefore I tell you, do not be anxious about your life, what you will eat or what you will drink, nor about your body, what you will put on. Is not life more than food, and the body more than clothing? Look at the birds of the air: they neither sow nor reap nor gather into barns, and yet your heavenly Father feeds them. Are you not of more value than they? And which of you by being anxious can add a single hour to his span of life? And why are you anxious about clothing? Consider the lilies of the field, how they grow: they neither toil nor spin, yet I tell you, even Solomon in all his glory was not arrayed like one of these. But if God so clothes the grass of the field, which today is alive and tomorrow is thrown into the oven, will he not much more*

clothe you, O you of little faith? Therefore do not be anxious, saying, 'What shall we eat?' or 'What shall we drink?' or 'What shall we wear?' For the Gentiles seek after all these things, and your heavenly Father knows that you need them all. But seek first the kingdom of God and his righteousness, and all these things will be added to you. "Therefore do not be anxious about tomorrow, for tomorrow will be anxious for itself. Sufficient for the day is its own trouble."

Matthew 6:25-34

Jesus is trying to tell his men that worry is wasted energy and effort altogether because, in the end, it's the Father that takes care of His children as he does for everything else. Furthermore, he says that it is the men of the world who run after all these things, not those who follow God. Those who don't know God ought to be the ones that worry because they don't have a Father who cares for them, who knows their needs and values them.

Real-World Testimony from the Apostle Paul

Paul knew what it was to experience extreme need and conversely have plenty in the bank. But he was confident in one thing: He could trust in God through every circumstance. This is even more extraordinary if you read of his real-life adventures in the book of Acts. Here is what he has to say in reflection on these adventures:

Not that I am speaking of being in need, for I have learned in whatever situation I am to be content. I know how to be brought low, and I know how to abound. In any and every circumstance, I have learned the secret of facing plenty and hunger, abundance and need. I can do all things through him who strengthens me.

Philippians 4:11-13

And then he adds confidence to this testimony for all men.

And my God will supply every need of yours according to his riches in glory in Christ Jesus.

Philippians 4:19

Every man will experience times of need and times of plenty. In either of these moments, we can live with confidence knowing that Jesus will meet our needs if we trust in Him. We can do all this through Him who gives us strength.

Here are three things we should remember about fear and faith.

One | Fear is evidence of unbelief.

First, fear of not having enough is a fear that springs from unbelief in God. As Jesus said, it is the "Fatherless men of the world" who run after stuff to satisfy their fear and anxiety, not men who call God their Father. It might be good to invest some time in reflecting on your unbelief when you experience fear about your needs or the future. It's this unbelief that drives our fear–name it and pray about it.

Two | Choose faith not unbelief.

Second, we must choose to be led by faith in God and not be led by our fears. Is this easy? Not always. But a journey of faith is a choice we must make daily and in each situation. If Paul could learn to trust God in the challenges of his circumstances, we can as well. When you feel your anxiety building, stop and ask yourself if you are living in belief or unbelief. Then recall worry is wasted energy and make the decision to not place trust in anything but God. As Jesus said, "Who of you by worrying can add a single hour to his life" - Matthew 6:27

Three | Ask for provision.

Third, ask God daily for provision in your unbelief. God is eager for us to ask Him for what we need. If we ask, He will respond. But He wants us to ask even though He already knows what we need. Jesus dares us to do this and promises God will provide for all our needs. "Ask, and it will be given to you; seek, and you will find; knock, and it will be opened to you." - Matthew 7:7

Remember, "Fatherless men" follow fear and unbelief. We follow our Father, and Him alone. Therefore, as a man with a Father, you should live free from fear because He loves you. He promises to care for you, which He repeats over and over in Scripture. In fact, the command for us to "fear not" is repeated 365 times, one for each day.

Reflection & Mentorship

Begin

- We need to trust God in moments of unbelief and fear.

Unpack

- How many men do you know who live anxious lives?
- What are we so anxious and fearful about?

Inform

"Therefore do not be anxious about tomorrow, for tomorrow will be anxious for itself. Sufficient for the day is its own trouble."

Matthew 6:25-34

- Put this phrase into your own words: "Tomorrow will be anxious for itself."
- Put this phrase into your own words: "Sufficient for the day is its own trouble."

Land

- What one fear or unbelief do you have?

Do

- Pray about this unbelief with a friend or mentor.
- Choose to daily give this unbelief to God and place your faith in Him.

The Enemy of Greed

"Greed, or avarice, is an inordinate or insatiable longing for material gain, be it food, money, status, or power. As a secular psychological concept, greed is an inordinate desire to acquire or possess more than one needs."

WIKIPEDIA

Greed! None of us like to think we are guilty of greed, but this is a struggle for many men, especially those of us who live in a consumer-captivated culture. Consider for just a moment all the things in your life that implore you for more. Are they not food, money, status, and power? Or consider the other side of the coin. What's your current level of contentment? Do you feel you have enough food, money, status, and power? As Wikipedia accurately states, we frequently want more, as these are everything a man wants.

Why Are Men Susceptible to Greed?

The primary reason greed is a problem is relatively simple. Men too often derive their significance from how they look, what they acquire, the status they attain, and the power they possess. Men will frequently compare the size of their house, the places they have eaten, the type of car they drive, and the salary they acquire with that of other men. And why? Well, because we think these things measure our influence, power, and ability. When this becomes a real problem, comparison ensues and results in us sizing up other men when we meet them. Even common introductions become assessments of a man's influence, power, and possession with one question: "What do you do for a living?" While many may intend the question to serve us as a casual conversation starter, the man controlled by greed may interpret this as a game of comparison rather than an honest gesture. For those excessively greedy, this is the first step to a means of domination and control of others.

Men will often give wealthy, financially, and powerful men more deference than those who have less of these resources. It is also why we have the desire to make more, acquire more, and possess more. It is as if life is a contest, and the one who wins has hoarded the most. When you think about that last statement, you realize how absurd it is, as we cannot take any of it with us. As the title of a book by John Ortberg says, "When the game is over, it all goes back in the box." At the end of life, none of our money, status, and power mean anything. Like a game of monopoly, the houses, dice, and money go back in the box at the end of the game.

The Source of our Value and Significance

So what gives us value?

If it is our stuff, power, or status, we are in deep trouble because things like these are assets that come and go. If you have ever lost your job and been unemployed for some time, you know how devastating that is to the male ego. For some men, it can feel as if we have lost our entire identity when all that's happened is we lost a source of income. These external factors are a powerful voice, and we allow them to speak to our significance and value. Yet this belief is an unbeliever's view of personal worth.

For the man of God, his accurate measure of our significance and self-worth is found in God's image and in Him alone. While that image was tarnished by sin, Jesus died to redeem it. God's gift in Jesus Christ demonstrates how deeply God values us. Because of that, we are now members and recipients of limitless resources, and we find value not in things–but in Him. Note what the apostle Paul says about our worth and value.

"But because of his great love for us, God, who is rich in mercy, made us alive with Christ even when we were dead in transgressions—it is by grace you have been saved. And God raised us up with Christ and seated us with him in the heavenly realms in Christ Jesus, in order that in the coming ages he might show the incomparable riches of his grace, expressed in his kindness to us in Christ Jesus. For it is by grace you have been saved, through faith—and this is not from yourselves, it is the gift of God—not by works, so that no one can boast. For we are God's handiwork, created in Christ Jesus to do good works, which God prepared in advance for us to do."

Ephesians 2:4-10

We are God's unique handiwork, created in Jesus to do good works that He prepared in advance for us to do. He saved us by grace for a purpose and imparted a value that comes not from ourselves or even all the good things we do. We, therefore, find our value only in Him, not the good we do, but the good God does, and this never ends.

The real value is eternal. Greed is not the path to significance but mercy, grace, forgiveness, faith, and God's good work in us.

Greed Is Out; Good Works Are In

Did you notice that we are "God's handiwork, created in Christ Jesus to do good works"? While the world focuses on money, status, and power to determine the value of our life's work, Jesus focuses on kingdom intangibles that advance His kingdom. And Christ wants us to use our gifts to help people on their journey for the benefit of leading people to Him, living out godly values in the marketplace, and bringing glory to his name–not greedily for self-advancement to build a legacy that will go back in the box.

Be careful not to let greed overtake you. But instead, let the desires of God consume you for the kingdom. Find your significance in Jesus and not in money, status, or power.

Reflection & Mentorship

Begin

- A man of God finds his identity not in the things of the world but in the things of God.

Unpack

- Is greed a problem for most men or not?
- What triggers greed for men?

Inform

For we are God's handiwork, created in Christ Jesus to do good works, which God prepared in advance for us to do."

Ephesians 2:4-10

- What image comes to mind when you hear the word "handiwork?"
- What does it mean to do "good works?"
- What are the consequences of "God preparing [us] in advance?"

Land

- What one thing do you need to do to address your greed?

Do

- Pray about that area in your life in which you are greedy.

Enough is Enough

Keep your lives free from the love of money and be content with what you have, because God has said, "Never will I leave you; never will I forsake you."

HEBREWS 13:5

A lifelong question every man must ask himself is, "How much is enough?" On the one hand, we have a deep drive to succeed, to set goals, and to accomplish great things in this life. On the other hand, we read in Scripture that we should have contentment that keeps our lives free from the love of money and excessive want that drives us to store possessions away into bigger barns.

How do we balance these two seemingly competing truths?

Here are several suggestions to consider.

One | Find Joy in Present Blessings.

Everyone also to whom God has given wealth and possessions and power to enjoy them, and to accept his lot and rejoice in his toil—this is the gift of God.

Ecclesiastes 5:19

The book of Ecclesiastes cites many times the value of hard work. It also tells us that we should enjoy the treasure God provides to each man. God wants us to both work with joy and even rejoice in it when we succeed. God rewards hard work done to honor Him.

Building a product or service that brings value to the world is noble in God's view. Work gives us a platform not only to contribute to society and provide for our family but to proclaim the good news to those around us for God's benefit. And we are encouraged to enjoy the gifts God graciously gives to us so the world will see our joy in Him. To not enjoy them is to miss the present blessings God wants us to enjoy and the potential for witness.

Two | Don't Love the Means.

He who loves money will not be satisfied with money, nor he who loves wealth with his income; this also is vanity.

Ecclesiastes 5:10

Money is not evil, but the love of money is the root of many evils. Money is only a means of exchange and nothing more. While we all need it, we are also tempted by it. It can become a temptation and, for some, a rival god in this life. Men over time will become drawn in and even intoxicated by its addictive nature, wanting more and more. But it's not money that is intoxicating–it is the things that money can get us, including possessions, power, and even the status it provides. This is what tempts men. This is what we must constantly consider during our lives. We must moderate this carefully because some men are so in love with possessions, power, and the status that money provides it keeps them from following Jesus enthusiastically–this was the case for many men in the Bible.

In the end, loving money is an insecure way to find security. We start pursuing money because of the security we think it provides. Over time, however, if we are not careful, our pursuit of possessions will possess us, and we will discover that we are reordering life around these resources. Our focus moves from believing in the person of Jesus to trusting in the pursuit of possessions and the power of money.

Three | Gauge Your Heart.

When goods increase, they increase who eat them, and what advantage has their owner but to see them with his eyes? Sweet is the sleep of a laborer, whether he eats little or much, but the full stomach of the rich will not let him sleep.

Ecclesiastes 5:11-12

Those who love money are never content. They will always want more and will make sacrifices to get more. We will even sacrifice marriage, children, and spiritual vitality to achieve the unachievable goal of more security and provision–trusting less in God for His provision and finding security in self. This accumulation of wealth is senseless.

So what can we do?

First, we need to practice daily contentment. Right now, even in your present circumstance, with your present status, power, and possessions. Learning contentment in your present situation will prepare you for those times of plenty or even want. When we learn to be faithful with little, God will make us faithful with lots. But if we don't learn contentment, the things of this life, like money, will possess us rather than us possessing them.

Second, give financially to God. Giving to God is a means of discipline, submission, and priority. It keeps us tuned to what is most important and helps us put God in the first position. Some call this tithing, which is an old biblical word. It means to set apart for God a portion of our first financial blessings. Tithing done regularly reminds us that God is responsible for all things, and He deserves to receive in accordance with the blessings he has given. After all, everything comes from God.

Third, consistently reject the world's beliefs about accumulation and wealth. In the book of Ecclesiastes, Solomon worked hard to teach us that wealth and the collection of wealth led to many issues. We need to reject the false beliefs we have about money since excess money has many dangers.

Fourth, remember your position is steward, not owner. Recalling regularly that we are mere stewards is crucial for us as men. God is the only owner. He owns all things and distributes as he sees fit. We are mere stewards in the story of God. Some men He allows to steward a lot, and some only a little. Regardless, steward it well and be content with the lot he has given.

In the end, we have a great God. He promises not to leave us or forsake us. So worry not; be content that the God who provides will provide.

Reflection & Mentorship

Begin

- Contentment is a practiced discipline in a man's life.

Unpack

- Do the men you know struggle with contentment?
- Do you find being content a challenge in the world today? Why?

Inform

Everyone also to whom God has given wealth and possessions and power to enjoy them, and to accept his lot and rejoice in his toil—this is the gift of God.

Ecclesiastes 5:19

- Who in the text above gives us wealth, possessions, and power?
- Why is it important to our contentment to learn to enjoy what we are given?
- If we don't learn to rejoice, what fails to happen?

Land

- Where do you experience a lack of contentment–money, possessions, or power?
- What issues make this a challenge for you?
- What steps do you need to take?

Do

- Talk with a friend or a mentor about the steps you need to take immediately.

Marketing Lies

The thief comes only to steal and kill and destroy. I came that they may have life and have it abundantly.

JOHN 10:10

The rich rules over the poor, and the borrower is the slave of the lender.

PROVERBS 22:7

I know how to be brought low, and I know how to abound. In any and every circumstance, I have learned the secret of facing plenty and hunger, abundance and need.

PHILIPPIANS 4:12

The marketing industry of the western world methodically devises ways daily to encourage men to spend money we don't have for products we usually don't need. They invest tons of money convincing us to spend more than we need to so we can have the most significant homes, the newest cars, the most elegant clothes, or a variety of other impulsive needs. And when we don't have the necessary funds for our chosen purchase, there is always credit to fall back on. They convince us to spend now, to save now, for something we want now, that we don't need now. And when the principal and interest on our credit becomes unbearable, there are always other consolidation loans to help us cope, driving up our fixed costs and scaling opportunities for more debt. It's the American way. When you take the time to think it over, you see how absurd the reasoning is.

Advertising Preys on Your Desire

There is a definitive connection between what the market communicates and our human desires. They may even know our desires more than we know our own. But the marketing industry cannot make us purchase something we don't desire. However, they can raise awareness of the fears we have to incite our want and desire.

Fear, or fear of missing out, is a common motivation for purchasing something right now. Fear may even prompt us to purchase a good or a service that we don't need, at the moment we don't need it, and at a price we shouldn't pay. For example, if we're afraid we'll miss out on a deal or experience, we may make that purchase today so we don't miss out on the opportunity in the future–even when we don't need it. Add a little greed to this fear, and it's a deadly combination. Now I don't know any man who would say that he is greedy. Yet every time we spend what we don't have and cannot afford, some sense of greed is driving us in cooperation with our fear. And remember, it's not the marketing industry convincing us–we are convincing ourselves, but our desires are carried away by the messages in combination with feelings of fear and greed.

Marketing Creates a Want in You

Marketing, most of the time, is generally truthful. But as accurate as it is, the bottom line of marketing is to sell a product. But remember that the object of marketing is usually not only to describe the product or service accurately but to sell something more profound–how their product or service will bring happiness to your life. Thus, in the process of selling their product, they must also clarify the need for the satisfaction you desire now.

In the desire to have something now, many end up finding a way to make a purchase today and then choose to put enormous and recurring purchases on credit cards. And this becomes fatal to a man's finances. In some cases, the promise of happiness is never delivered. It may suffice for a time, but when financial reality sets in, years of unhappy economic captivity are the result.

We must remember that products and services cannot bring us lasting happiness - only Jesus can provide permanent and eternal fulfillment. It is our responsibility to understand the underlying message of marketing and the true nature of freedom and happiness, which includes avoiding the financial pressure to accrue debt.

Scripture Gives Significant Financial Advice

Jesus, in our verse above, made it clear that only He could give real life and life in all its fullness. The same verse states that the thief is one who comes to steal, kill, and destroy. Financial bondage is one means of stealing, killing, and destroying our life. We need to ask ourselves where we are looking for fulfillment and meaning in life prior to accruing mass amounts of debt. If we are looking for fulfillment in stuff, then we are on the wrong path.

Our proverb above states that those who borrow become the slave of the lenders. No one wants to be a slave to another, but that is precisely what we do when we buy into the message of marketing too quickly.

Then there is the warning from Paul above in which he shares his conviction about contentment regardless of circumstances. Interestingly, Paul said he had "learned to be content" in both good times and hard times. Contentment is something we should all learn. Marketers might dislike this, but contented men will not fall for the lie and the promise of happiness.

Don't Buy the Lie

The lie that stuff brings us happiness is false. It is not valid. Start listening critically to the advertising you hear and see and are bombarded with hundreds of times a day. Think about the underlying message and ask if it is true. Consider whether you can afford what they are selling, if you need it, and whether a purchase will help or hurt your financial peace and ability to please God with your resources. Don't be fooled and don't be foolish.

Reflection & Mentorship

Begin

- We must be careful and watchful and not fall for the lies sold to us by popular marketing.

Unpack

- Have you ever purchased something you did not need? Why did you?
- Do you pay attention to the "happiness messages" that products and services promise? Do any really grab your attention that do a good job of selling to you?

Inform

The thief comes only to steal and kill and destroy. I came that they may have life and have it abundantly.

John 10:10

The rich rules over the poor, and the borrower is the slave of the lender.

Proverbs 22:7

I know how to be brought low, and I know how to abound. In any and every circumstance, I have learned the secret of facing plenty and hunger, abundance and need.

Philippians 4:12

- Who is real abundant life found in? Do we believe this in our "want more" world?
- "Borrower is a slave to the lender." This is strong language, is it true? How so?
- Over time and experience, we can learn contentment as Paul talks about. What great lessons have you learned about being content?

Land

- What issues make marketing a challenge for you?
- What steps do you need to take?

Do

- Talk with a friend or a mentor about the steps you need to take immediately.

Owners or Stewards

"Teacher, which is the great commandment in the Law?" And he said to him, "You shall love the Lord your God with all your heart and with all your soul and with all your mind. This is the great and first commandment.

MATTHEW 22:36-38

And the Lord said, "Who then is the faithful and wise manager, whom his master will set over his household, to give them their portion of food at the proper time? Blessed is that servant whom his master will find so doing when he comes.

LUKE 12:42-43

A major shift occurs in a man's spiritual life when he discovers that giving everything to Christ means we must be willing to give everything, anything, and all things to Him. We cease to be owners but instead become stewards. We steward God's resources on behalf of God who is the one who owns all things.

Stewardship Changes Our Mindset

When we take on the identity of a steward, our title, position, and responsibilities change with it. This includes how we interpret money and possessions. But pre-Christ, we did not view things this way. We used to be of the mindset that what we do possess does belong to us and can be used at our discretion and for our pleasure. The only constraints on how we used and distributed our wealth were our personal priorities. It was ours and we could do with it what we saw fit.

But when we give our lives to Christ, we give Christ everything. We pledge to give our heart, mind, soul, and strength to God and love Him first before all other things–this includes money. And we must come to terms with the fact that everything we have is no longer ours but God, including "our" money. I use the term "our" loosely here; this may be the incorrect pronoun to use for the Christian man. We may hold money, we may bank money, we may spend money, but it actually no longer belongs to us but to God. We are only a steward, not an owner, like we once thought we were. We are placed in a temporary stewardship/management role to oversee its use and impact and use it to yield kingdom purposes.

The Practices of a Steward

It is far more challenging to positionally be a steward than it is to be an owner. This is clearly so because it implies an understanding and ongoing accountability for fulfilling the wishes of the owner. The owner in this case is only God. To fulfill our role as stewards, we must adhere to certain behaviors.

First, stewards know the priorities of the owner. They have a mind for what is important to the owner. In our case, that means that we understand the financial principles and priorities of God who gave us the opportunity to steward what we have been given. God is the source for all truth, even the truth about money. He is the first owner, and only owner, and He sets the rules. We have a responsibility to learn the principles of money through the teaching of great men in God's Word like King Solomon or even the several stories Jesus tells in the New Testament about money. We should read, learn, and adhere to these principles.

Second, stewards avoid cultural pitfalls when it comes to spending, investing, and saving money. Most of us have dreams and desires but fail to talk with Jesus first about our desires prior to spending, investing, and saving. Instead, it is easy to be impulsive, ignore godly desires, and fall into the ditch of debt seeking immediate satisfaction. If we had simply sought God first, we would have been spared pain. If our possessions are actually God's, it goes without saying that we would talk to him first about how we would like to use them and spend less time seeking forgiveness and more time asking permission.

Third, a steward makes smarter choices over time. As we mature in our faith and followership, this becomes easier since we get to know God better through the Word and maybe many mistakes. A good best practice is to invest time in prayer before any purchase of $50 or more. Just take a second to pray about it, and you'll discover that your heart will align with God's. You may even walk right out of the store or wait till later. God may even reveal a principle that He calls to your mind.

The Triple Bottom Line

Think about this: There are only a few things that cross the line from time into eternity. First, our decision to follow Christ, based on God's grace. Second, the people we have spiritually invested in who have also crossed the line of faith. Third, the financial investments which have resulted in kingdom advancement during our lifetime.

Here is the deal. You can take none of your stuff with you into eternity, but you can use it to contribute to the storehouses of heaven. We "store up treasures in heaven" when we invest in ministries that advance the gospel, whether evangelism, our local church, mission work, or compassion work done in the name of Jesus.

Those who steward their resources on behalf of Christ truly witness the impact of godly stewardship. What we have is not our own. We merely steward it for a short time, but how we do this has eternal implications. We allow God to transform us as we work to be involved in the spiritual transformation of others and make financial investments in ministries that reach those we cannot reach. When you look at life that way, you realize it is all about Jesus - and His priorities for our lives.

Reflection & Mentorship

Begin

- We are merely stewards in this life, and that has implications.

Unpack

- Is it hard to move from the mentality of owner to steward for men? Why or why not?
- How have you made this transition in your mindset?

Inform

"Teacher, which is the great commandment in the Law?" And he said to him, "You shall love the Lord your God with all your heart and with all your soul and with all your mind. This is the great and first commandment.

Matthew 22:36-38

And the Lord said, "Who then is the faithful and wise manager, whom his master will set over his household, to give them their portion of food at the proper time? Blessed is that servant whom his master will find so doing when he comes.

Luke 12:42-43

- The great commandment is perhaps one of the hardest to obey. Can we really love God with all our heart, soul, and mind in this life? Do you feel you do?
- Managers and stewards were synonymous ideas. What has God set you over to manage?

Land

- What daily steps do you need to take to remember that you are a steward and not an owner?

Do

- Take a daily step this week to be the steward and notice how God uses you.

Comparison Helps and Hurts

Not that we dare to classify or compare ourselves with some of those who are commending themselves. But when they measure themselves by one another and compare themselves with one another, they are without understanding.

2 CORINTHIANS 10:12

It feels like men were made to compare themselves with other men. We compare just about everything: homes, cars, titles, power, money, toys, physiques, and all kinds of other things. It feels like it was built into our nature. We don't do it exactly the same way women do, but still, we do it.

Comparison Can Be Helpful

One way men learn is through healthy comparison. We might even learn best by watching others and how they do what they do. We are not great at asking for directions, but we do try to learn from other men we believe are successful, skillful, and who we respect. Just as we watched our fathers and learned from them (for good or ill), we do the same thing with other men.

For example, we may compare our spending patterns with those around us and realize some men are willing to live more modestly than us, and yet they seem perfectly satisfied. In addition, they seem less financially stressed and strapped. You may learn from discussions or even time with them that they defer purchases until they can pay them with cash rather than credit. This comparison can make us better financial stewards. There are several examples, but the point is that some natural comparisons can direct us toward positive and God-honoring behaviors.

Comparison Can Be Mistaken

It is also easy to assume that when those around us seem to have more or better, we have somehow missed the boat. Sometimes we feel that we deserve what they have. Or that if they can buy the best and the newest, we can too—even if it means using credit and leveraging our finances to get there. Men are very easily influenced by the other men around them.

Here is what you need to remember. Those who spend freely and seem to have a lot are not necessarily living wisely or responsibly, and their decisions should not be your decisions.

A friend told me the story of a successful stockbroker who always had a dozen of the best vehicles, multiple homes, took several vacations each year, had a yacht in Florida, and had an endless supply of cash. He had a string of seemingly successful investment positions and was the major stockbroker in his town. It was easy, said my friend, to look at him with envy. After all, this guy was no smarter than he, but he seemed to have arrived at the top of the financial ladder. Then one day he was forced to file for bankruptcy. His first home was mortgaged at 700,000 but was worth 500,000, so he couldn't sell it. His yacht was repossessed for back payment. His second home was repossessed as well since he had not been paying the mortgage. He had lived large but was, in fact, worth nothing or less than nothing. My friend of modest means realized soon after his fall from glory that he actually had more assets than his "wealthy" friend who had been living on credit and debt.

Comparison Can Be Hurtful

There is a downside to comparison because it can lead to the temptation of believing we are better than others. Sometimes we engage in comparison because we want to one-up someone else. To make ourselves feel better about self, we compare our lives unfairly with others. We may think we are "not like them" or "not as bad them." This type of comparison is a subtle form of self-elevation. When we do this, as Paul said above in 2 Corinthians, we are "without understanding." Simply put, we are foolish to do this. Measuring ourselves by others for this purpose is not only hurtful of others, but it's hurtful of self, for we choose to live in a state of self-deception. This comparison can result in deep hurt.

The Productive Comparison

Comparisons, however, can be helpful when done from the right motivation - if our goal is to find ways to live more wisely, especially in the area of finances. At the end of our lives, the wise comparisons and resultant wise financial decisions will ultimately lead to happiness. The only comparison we should be making regularly is our financial habits as compared to what the Scriptures teach about money.

No one can serve two masters, for either he will hate the one and love the other, or he will be devoted to the one and despise the other. You cannot serve God and money.

Matthew 6:24

Acquire no gold or silver or copper for your belts, no bag for your journey, or two tunics or sandals or a staff, for the laborer deserves his food.

Matthew 10:9-10

For the love of money is a root of all kinds of evils. It is through this craving that some have wandered away from the faith and pierced themselves with many pangs.

1 Timothy 6:10

Reflection & Mentorship

Begin

- Comparison can help or hurt, but it must done from the right motivation.

Unpack

- Do men tend to make healthy or hurtful comparisons?
- How about you? Are your comparisons truly done in a helpful way?

Inform

Not that we dare to classify or compare ourselves with some of those who are commending themselves. But when they measure themselves by one another and compare themselves with one another, they are without understanding.

2 Corinthians 10:12

- Paul is talking about making spiritual comparisons to feel self-righteous. Can we be self-righteous about our money?
- What common language could replace the phrase "they are without understanding."

Land

- How could you choose to use comparisons more appropriately?
- What steps do you need to take to do this?

Do

- Take action.

Money Management

There's a right way and a wrong way to manage resources that belong to someone else. In "The Parable of the Dishonest Manager," Jesus uses a negative example to drive home a few positive points about being a good steward and a great manager. "But how is this relevant to me?" some of you might ask. "I really don't manage anybody's money or resources but my own." Just keep in mind that as followers of Christ, we know everything belongs to God. We are given the opportunity to manage the resources God has entrusted to us for a short while. Below, we break down the story and discover a few lessons we can learn from it.

Lesson One | Stop Wasting.

"There was a rich man who had a manager, and charges were brought to him that this man was wasting his possessions."

Luke 16:1

"Wasting" is a loaded term here. This manager was being charged with more than just frivolous spending. Later in the story, he is called a "dishonest" manager. Apparently, he was siphoning off a little extra cash for himself, maybe padding his commission a little.

We are called to be scrupulously honest about everything God gives us to manage, even the seemingly little things. There's a lot of blind eyes turned at taking office supplies, showing up late, or using work time for personal endeavors, for example. Don't be trapped by the "Oh, they'll never know" lie. Be honest with your employer, with yourself, and with God. No exceptions. Ever.

Lesson Two | Be accountable.

"And he called him and said to him, 'What is this that I hear about you? Turn in the account of your management, for you can no longer be manager.'"

Luke 16:2

This dishonest manager got caught and he got fired. In his arrogance, he missed the fact that someone, somewhere, was holding him accountable nonetheless. Ultimately, we are accountable to God, of course, and He knows everything. Ask God to examine your heart and eliminate any selfish motives or shifty tendencies. With God's help, be above reproach in everything. Engage others to help hold you accountable and be sure you have nothing to hide.

Lesson Three | Plan Wisely.

"And the manager said to himself, 'What shall I do, since my master is taking the management away from me? I am not strong enough to dig, and I am ashamed to beg. I have decided what to do, so that when I am removed from management, people may receive me into their houses.'"

Luke 16:3-4

The now unemployed manager had to step back and learn from his mistakes. What might he do to regain trust and rebuild his reputation? What are you doing to maintain the trust of others and preserve or even improve your own reputation? It takes thought, intentionality, discipline (with the Holy Spirit's help!), and a generous dose of wisdom from God's Word—not just in good stewardship but also life in general.

Lesson Four: Be Shrewd.

"So, summoning his master's debtors one by one, he said to the first, 'How much do you owe my master?' He said, 'A hundred measures of oil.' He said to him, 'Take your bill, and sit down quickly and write fifty.' Then he said to another, 'And how much do you owe?' He said, 'A hundred measures of wheat.' He said to him, 'Take your bill, and write eighty.' The master commended the dishonest manager for his shrewdness."

Luke 16:5-9

In other words, be strategic. Think ahead. Invest a little now to gain more later. Seek God's guidance for the best courses of action. Get advice from other brothers and sisters you trust. What's fair? How might everyone concerned come out ahead? There's a big "don't" in there, too: don't be greedy!

"One who is faithful in a very little is also faithful in much, and one who is dishonest in a very little is also dishonest in much. If then you have not been faithful in the unrighteous wealth, who will entrust to you the true riches? And if you have not been faithful in that which is another's, who will give you that which is your own? No servant can serve two masters, for either he will hate the one and love the other, or he will be devoted to the one and despise the other. You cannot serve God and money."

Luke 16:10-13

Jesus concludes His tutorial in money management with some hard-hitting questions and an uncompromising statement of truth. Take stock. Have you been honest? Have you been faithful? Who's your master? Let us make the commitment and renew it daily to serve no thing and no one else but God.

Reflection & Mentorship

Begin

- There is a right way and a dishonest way to manage our money.

Unpack

- When you hear the word management, what comes to mind?
- How would you define mismanagement?

Inform

- Of the four lessons above, which is the most challenging for you?
- Is there one lesson that comes easier for you? Explain why?

Land

- What issue do you need to address?
- What actionable steps do you need to take?

Do

- Take a step of action this week based on the decisions above.

Rich Words to the Wise

There's no better source of wisdom about money than from a really rich man like Solomon. He is consistently referenced in the Bible as the wealthiest and wisest man to ever live. When as a young man Solomon told God that he desired wisdom more than anything else, God granted him both wisdom and riches—and his wealth was astounding even by today's standards. In the book of Proverbs, we have access to a wealth of Solomon's wisdom—inspired by God and timeless in its relevance.

Here are three nuggets that will help us to be wise about money.

One | Know when to quit.

> *"Do not toil to acquire wealth; be discerning enough to desist. When your eyes light on it, it is gone, for suddenly it sprouts wings, flying like an eagle toward heaven."*
>
> Proverbs 23:4-5

God is not telling us, here, that we shouldn't work to make a living. Rather, He is telling us not to wear ourselves out piling up wealth. Simply put, we need to recognize when enough is enough. As good stewards of the financial and material resources God has assigned to our care, we do indeed want to provide for our families, pay our bills, and give to those who need it. But spending time and effort acquiring wealth for wealth's sake is foolish. It accomplishes nothing—and in a flash, it can all be carried away.

Two | Check your motives for making a profit.

"A good man leaves an inheritance to his children's children, but the sinner's wealth is laid up for the righteous."

Proverbs 13:22

Be sure that when you seek financial gain, your methods and motives are pure. It's fine to save a little honest pay for honest work to one day benefit your kids and grandkids. Whatever wealth you might leave behind when you go home to heaven will land with your heirs. But God's justice ultimately is served one way or another. The warning here is that a man's ill-gotten gain will eventually end up in the hands of the "good guys" anyway, rather than remain in his own possession or the possession of his family.

Three | Honesty is the best policy.

"Wealth gained hastily will dwindle, but whoever gathers little by little will increase it."

Proverbs 13:11

Here we find yet another admonishment not only to be honest in the way we earn an income but also the patience required. In this context, "hastily" can infer dishonestly gained or even quickly gained–as from winning a bet or benefitting from some sort of windfall. But don't be confused. Sometimes God blesses us with an occasional windfall–an inheritance, perhaps, or a gift from a friend–and that's okay. Gambling, on the other hand, doesn't really fit God's parameters for good, honest ways to make a living. The point, though, is that sudden gains seem to slip through our fingers quicker than the income we earn over time through honest labor. Perhaps we tend to be more careful about how we budget it, spend it, and invest it. Even more to the point–we must never count on sudden gains to get us by. We acquire a more dependable, long-lasting income through being patient.

Proverbs is a goldmine of God-inspired wisdom about money and life right at our fingertips. Read it and treasure it.

"Your Word is a lamp to my feet and a light to my path."

Psalm 119:105

Reflection & Mentorship

Begin

- Solomon, the wisest and wealthiest man to ever live, has lots to say about how we handle our money.

Unpack

- Do you ever feel like money goes out faster than it comes in?
- Who do you go to when looking for wisdom about money?

Inform

- Of the three lessons of Solomon above, which one captures your attention?
- What does Solomon's wisdom teach you about your money issues?

Land

- What issue do you need to address?
- What would happen if you successfully addressed these issues?

Do

- Take a step of action this week based on the decisions above.

Living on a Budget

The word "budget" can conjure up some negative thoughts and attitudes for men. We frequently think about denying ourselves, limiting our lifestyle, and delaying gratification by means of discipline. And we live in a time where instant gratification is socially acceptable and even endorsed. However, the pain of indiscipline in our financial affairs is far greater than discovering the discipline of living on a budget.

The Cost of Financial Carelessness

No man starts life with dreams of living in financial devastation. This would be sheer insanity. More often than not, the issue is simply carelessness. It is too easy to think things will take care of themselves, and since immediate gratification is acceptable, we think putting another purchase on the card is fine. But paying off these lines of credit with high interest is never easy. Pretty soon, we look up to see bills stacked up in front of us only to feel robbed of the pleasure we sought. And soon we are in financial bondage.

What Is a Budget?

A budget is a plan for managing our financial resources. Anything of importance requires a plan, and that is what a budget is. One benefit of a budget is that you visually see what your monthly income and monthly fixed expenses are. After writing it all down for the first time, you may be surprised. There are all kinds of tools for making this easy for you, but just making a list helps. It's important to be honest about what you are spending, particularly in non-fixed costs such as entertainment, meals out, and other similar items.

Once you understand your spending, you can make other allocations. Keep in mind giving to the church, which is called a tithe and is 10 percent. Consider putting some into a basic savings account, typically an additional 10 percent. All this means that your fixed and non-fixed expenses must be equal to or less than the remaining 80 percent, which is yours to spend as you see fit monthly. It is unwise not to give or save, even if you think you can go without allocating a budget to these items.

Next, the real budgeting work begins, especially if the 80 percent exceeds your current spending patterns. You cannot spend more than you take in, so you must make choices at this point about what expenses need to be modified, eliminated, or reigned in. If you are having a hard time making this work, then you may need to get some financial accountability from another Christian man or family member.

Here are a few budgeting principles to live by:

- As Christ followers, God comes first. The first 10 percent of your income goes to Him and is not available for other expenses.
- As responsible people, the second 10 percent goes to your savings. It is irresponsible to be unprepared for unexpected expenses.
- All other expenses must come from the remaining 80 percent, which will require monitoring and discipline on a daily, weekly, and monthly basis.
- It is important to have a monthly discussion with your spouse (if married) to review your financial end game. Did you keep your budget, and if not, what must you adjust the following month to do so? You may need to

address some expenses that caused you to go over your budgeted allocations. Don't neglect a check-in. Budgets don't mean anything if they are not monitored, called into accountability, and even adjusted when necessary.
- Get some counsel from a trusted friend or mentor about their budgeting process. There is wisdom in many godly counselors.
- Learn to be content with what God has given you. Don't look at others and what they have. In fact, many of your friends are probably seriously in debt because of their spending.
- Learn to trust God for His provision. He owns everything and will meet your true needs if you ask and are obedient to His truth.

Like many things in life, budgeting and living with a little discipline are one route to peace and joy. Choose peace and joy over instant gratification and you will be blessed for doing so.

> *"One who is faithful in a very little is also faithful in much, and one who is dishonest in a very little is also dishonest in much. If then you have not been faithful in the unrighteous wealth, who will entrust to you the true riches? And if you have not been faithful in that which is another's, who will give you that which is your own?*
>
> Luke 16:10-12

Reflection & Mentorship

Begin

- Budgeting is a discipline required of faithful men.

Unpack

- Has anyone ever taught you to budget?
- What budgeting principle do you live by?

Inform

"One who is faithful in a very little is also faithful in much, and one who is dishonest in a very little is also dishonest in much. If then you have not been faithful in the unrighteous wealth, who will entrust to you the true riches? And if you have not been faithful in that which is another's, who will give you that which is your own?

Luke 16:10-12

- What does it mean to learn to be "faithful in unrighteous wealth"?
- What could "true riches" be referring to in this text?

Land

- What prevents you from budgeting?
- What do you need to address to be more faithful in your budgeting?

Do

- Develop a budget and stick with it for three months and then share what you learn.

Owing Is Slavery

Rather go to bed without dinner than to rise in debt.

BENJAMIN FRANKLIN

How much money do you owe? Most Americans carry some debt, and that's not including home mortgages. The stats are alarming. More to the point, how does your debt make you feel? Stressed? Suffocated? Enslaved? You're not alone, brother! I believe we can all agree that debt is not our friend. Indeed, it's an enemy. But knowing the enemy can better equip us to defeat it. So let's look at a few choice bits of wisdom about debt from God's Word.

One | Debt is financial slavery.

"The rich rules over the poor, and the borrower is the slave of the lender."

Proverbs 22:7

The very second you borrow money, you are burdened with an obligation to pay it back. And this obligation carries weight–it adds to your load. It means you've already spent money you don't even have yet, and life lived this way is defeating. Suddenly, you must add another item to your list of bills and then exercise the discipline to pay back a portion of it from every paycheck. Face it–you're a slave.

Two | We owe enough already.

"Pay to all what is owed to them: taxes to whom taxes are owed, revenue to whom revenue is owed, respect to whom respect is owed, honor to whom honor is owed."

Romans 13:7

It's not a sin to have expenses. We all have them. Every month we pay taxes, utility bills, insurance premiums, service fees, and the list goes on. We owe substantial sums of money already without adding debt to the picture. Who needs that? So pay what you owe and stop accruing unneeded debt.

Three | Debt is a sign you love something too much.

"No one can serve two masters, for either he will hate the one and love the other, or he will be devoted to the one and despise the other. You cannot serve God and money."

Matthew 6:24

Don't fool yourself into believing that we actually can serve two masters. Isn't it possible to rack up the debt and still put God first? Nope. Won't happen. Debt is distracting. It's bothersome. It occupies the mind and sort of shoves everything else aside. It doesn't help that our culture encourages an attitude of entitlement and a mindset of instant gratification. Sure, it's okay to look forward to a new purchase of some kind, but first, we need to assign it the appropriate priority in our budget, save for it, and patiently wait for it until we can pay for it. It's called living within our means. And sometimes after we've waited a while, we realize we don't really want or need this new thing after all!

Four | There is one debt you can owe.

"Owe no one anything, except to love each other."

Romans 13:8

Love each other. Now there's a debt we can afford and embrace. We owe it to our family, friends, neighbors, co-workers–indeed everyone in our circles of influence–to love them, even those we find hard to love. It's a debt God actually sanctions. In fact, He commands it. But in a very real sense, to love is more of an investment than a debt. The more we love, the more our capacity to love grows. So I guess the moral of the story is "Be free from debt and love freely."

A Final Word

Whether or not you have any debt, seek God's guidance to establish a budget and stick to it. Figure out how much of your monthly income you'll need to spend on each budget item and be disciplined about adhering to your plan. Be sure to give back to God first–your giving should top the list. And don't add to your debt. Rather, whittle it down until there's none left. Got more expenses than funds? Then cut back your spending wherever possible and increase your income. Not easy, I know, but it is that simple. Trust me. Better yet, trust God. Between you and Him, you've got this.

Reflection & Mentorship

Begin

- Owing money to anyone is a form of enslavement.

Unpack

- How much debt do you think the average American accrues during their lifetime?

- Why do we live with this much debt?

Inform

- Which of the four Scriptures above most convicts you? Why?
- What lesson from this text do you need to embrace?

Land

- What practical steps do you need to take?

Do

- What one thing do you need to stop being enslaved to lenders?

The Problem with Treasure

What does the Bible really say about treasure? Is it good or bad?

On the one hand, Proverbs 13:22 says that "a good man leaves an inheritance to his children's children." On the other hand, 1 Timothy 6:10 says that the "love of money is a root of all kinds of evils." So should we have treasure or not? Let's look at four biblical truths about treasure for some answers.

One | Treasure is a matter of the heart.

"For where your treasure is, there will your heart be also."

Luke 12:34

Treasure is something you cherish, something you hold dear, something you value. You could even say that it's something you love. So it makes sense to say that "where your treasure is, there will your heart be also." There's no great mystery here. The greatest treasure in your life is defined by what you love the most. And of course, as followers of Christ, we seek to love God first and foremost. We treasure our relationship with Him, and that's a treasure worth having.

Two | Treasures reside in two places, and in one they last forever.

"Do not lay up for yourselves treasures on earth, where moth and rust destroy and where thieves break in and steal, but lay up for yourselves treasures in heaven, where neither moth nor rust destroys and where thieves do not break in and steal."

Matthew 6:19-20

There are treasures on earth and treasures in heaven. Treasures on earth don't last. Treasures in heaven last forever. Which would you rather lay up for yourself? It's a no-brainer. We can put on a show of righteousness here on earth in order to get noticed and praised by others–and that is the extent of our reward. Or we can humbly and quietly serve God, seek to glorify Him, share the good news of Christ with others–all motivated by our love for Him–and He will reward us with treasure in heaven. We have to wait for it, but it will last forever.

Three | Heaven is a treasure worth buying.

"The kingdom of heaven is like treasure hidden in a field, which a man found and covered up. Then in his joy he goes and sells all that he has and buys that field."

Matthew 13:44

The point here has nothing to do with the man re-hiding the treasure in the field before buying the plot of land. The point is that the kingdom of heaven is worth giving up everything you have in order to get there. It's our inheritance, and absolutely nothing on earth–no amount of wealth or material possessions–can compare to what God has laid up for us in heaven.

Four | Sometimes real treasure costs everything.

"Jesus said to him, 'If you would be perfect, go, sell what you possess and give to the poor, and you will have treasure in heaven; and come, follow me.'"

Matthew 19:21

Indeed, laying up treasure in heaven might mean significant sacrifice here on earth, but it's a trade worth making. Why would you not trade your prized agate marble when you know that in return, you'll receive a priceless diamond? It's not a perfect analogy, but I think you get my drift.

Our motivation, of course, should not be greed, or to see whose pile of treasure in heaven stacks the highest. Instead, let our motivation be our love for Jesus and our gratitude for the supreme sacrifice He made for us on the cross. After all, there is no greater treasure than knowing we are children of God—co-heirs with Christ who are destined to spend eternity with Him in Paradise.

Reflection & Mentorship

Begin

- We should seek treasure as long as it's the right kind of treasure.

Unpack

- What do you treasure here on earth? Why is this so?
- What do you treasure about heaven? Why is this so?

Inform

- Which of the four Scriptures above is the most challenging? Why?

- What lesson does this Scripture teach?

Land

- What step do you need to take to pursue the right kind of treasure?

Do

- Give up one thing for God.

The Lack Mindset

For me, all my negative thoughts that I have about, "How did you miss that pitch? Why did you miss that pitch? You shouldn't have missed that pitch." I just kind of sit there and kind of crush it up, and once I'm done doing that... I just kind of toss it aside.

AARON JUDGE

Money matters, but not so much the way you might think. Yes, it's true that in most cultures around the world, people are paid for their work with some form of currency. We use currency to buy food, get clothing, and provide shelter. We exchange it to get our needs met.

But money matters in a much different and more insidious way too. It can trip a guy up. It can become an all-consuming object of desire and greed that leads to corruption, ruin, and evil. And just when you think I am overstating the case, you quickly realize that I am not. Note what Scripture says:

"For the love of money is a root of all kinds of evils. It is through this craving that some have wandered away from the faith and pierced themselves with many pangs."

1 Timothy 6:10

No wonder the Bible mentions money so often–by one count, there are more than 2,300 verses about money, wealth, and possessions.

The FOMO Factor

It's not that money in and of itself is terrible. It's only an object and a tool. It's a resource God wants us to manage well. Invested, spent, and used wisely, money can aid the poor, feed the hungry, and go a long way toward helping spread the good news of the gospel and building God's kingdom. The thing that gets us in trouble, though, is when we start believing that we don't or will never have enough of it. I call it "The Lack Mindset." Admit it. How often do you catch yourself thinking, "If only I had a little more cash..."?

And our culture doesn't help matters any. We are bombarded day in and day out with appeals from all types of media trying to convince us that we need nicer cars, bigger houses, better clothes, and more luxurious vacations. The result? Wanting. Craving. FOMO, or fear of missing out. The temptation to love money can be overwhelming.

Fear No More

So let's be sure right off the bat that we adopt the right attitude about money and things and material possessions.

Here are three perspectives that will keep us on the right track.

One | Trust in God, not your stuff.

Easier said than done, I know, but think about it. We're always looking for "the sure thing," right? The only thing that's "sure" about your stuff, however, is that it's temporary. It's subject to age and decay. It can be taken away in an instant. God, on the other hand, is eternal. He is unchanging, ever loving and ever gracious.

"Trust in the Lord with all your heart, and do not lean on your own understanding."

Proverbs 3:5

We may not always understand His ways (how can we? He's God, and we're not), but we know we can always, always trust Him.

Two | Accept that you have already been given everything.

Really, now, what more could we want? The keys to a new car or the keys to heaven–eternity in paradise with God Himself? The truth is that in Christ, we have hit the biggest jackpot of all. And money can't buy it. Jesus bought it with His blood, and all we have to do is accept it.

"Blessed be the God and Father of our Lord Jesus Christ, who has blessed us in Christ with every spiritual blessing in the heavenly places."

Ephesians 1:3

Three | Invest your time in real treasures that don't depreciate or demand more.

One of the great things about the tremendous wealth we have as co-heirs with Christ is that when we share it, spread it around, and give it away, not one iota is subtracted from our inheritance. In fact, we end up adding to the treasure God is safeguarding for us in heaven.

"Do not lay up for yourselves treasures on earth, where moth and rust destroy and where thieves break in and steal, but lay up for yourselves treasures in heaven, where neither moth nor rust destroys and where

thieves do not break in and steal. For where your treasure is, there your heart will be also."

Matthew 6:19-21

Where is your heart? We work hard to earn a living and pay the bills. But when we hit a low spot, and we're unsure how to fund our next meal, we are only reminded of how fleeting our wealth here on earth is. Yes, money matters. Let's make sure that it matters for the Kingdom of God.

Reflection & Mentorship

Begin

- A lack mindset can trip men up if we are not careful.

Unpack

- Do you agree that humanity tends to have a lack mindset?
- When does this lack mindset become motivationally dangerous to a man's faith? Is there a specific tipping point?

Inform

"Do not lay up for yourselves treasures on earth, where moth and rust destroy and where thieves break in and steal, but lay up for yourselves treasures in heaven, where neither moth nor rust destroys and where thieves do not break in and steal. For where your treasure is, there your heart will be also."

Matthew 6:19-21

- This verse differentiates between earthly and heavenly treasures. What are the differences between them?

- What do our treasures communicate about our motivation? Have you ever thought about this before?

Land

- How do you get your motivations to line up with heavenly investments and treasures?
- What is preventing you from doing this today?

Do

- Take one step of obedience toward investing in something of eternal value and share the experience with someone else.

Retirement Plans

Often when you think you're at the end of something, you're at the beginning of something else.

FRED ROGERS

Retirement can be a touchy topic in some circles, so let's be clear about one thing right up front—we never retire from doing the work of the Lord. We might retire from a vocation, but as followers of Christ, we continue to serve God's purposes for our lives here on earth until the day we die.

That said, I'll make what should be a rather obvious observation: we must steward our financial resources well, not from a worldly perspective, but a biblical perspective.

It's All God's

Being a steward means managing something that belongs to someone else. Whatever your emotional attachment might be to your wealth and material possessions, the bottom line is this—God owns it all. Everything. And He is clear in Scripture that we will occasionally encounter some thin times. So we must be shrewd in stewarding what belongs to Him.

Here are three principles that will aid us immeasurably in the stewardship of God's resources.

One | Avoid worshiping some future state (of anything, including ease).

But I do not account my life of any value nor as precious to myself, if only I may finish my course and the ministry that I received from the Lord Jesus, to testify to the gospel of the grace of God.

Acts 20:24

Paul is sharing from his heart above about what he deems most valuable: the story of God's grace in his life. And Paul knows something about grace. He knows a lot about it. Just consider the man he used to be. He was known as a cruel persecutor of Christians, and he was consumed with it. We, too, can become so obsessed with money that we worship it and the things we invest it in. We can even do this with retirement and the things it provides, including ease and comfort. We can become consumed with the kind of lifestyle we want for ourselves with all of its perks and pleasures. But of course, Scripture tells us that He and He alone is worthy of our worship, and ease and comfort are not the focus of our worship, nor are they guaranteed on this side of heaven. Paul states that even his life is not precious to himself, which is evidence of his real investment. What is he investing in? His testimony "to the gospel of grace."

Two | We never retire – only our duties change.

And the Lord spoke to Moses, saying," This applies to the Levites: from 25-years-old, and upward they shall come to do duty in the service of the tent of meeting. And from the age of 50 years they shall withdraw from the duty of the service and serve no more."

Number 8:23-24

Indeed, our duties will change over time–our call to service will look different in each stage. But this does not mean we end up just sitting on the bench and removing ourselves from the game. Never! Men at age fifty in Israel became the most useful mentors and leaders. Even Moses at this time was well into his hundreds, and he was very useful to God more during his 80-120-year range than ever before.

What is your call to service at this time in your life? Indeed, one responsibility we have or will have as we gain more life experience is to mentor the next generation and prepare them for a life of service in the kingdom.

Three | The timeline is uncertain, and storing up more may be the wrong choice.

And he told them a parable, saying, "The land of a rich man produced plentifully, and he thought to himself, 'What shall I do, for I have nowhere to store my crops?' And he said, 'I will do this: I will tear down my barns and build larger ones, and there I will store all my grain and my goods. And I will say to my soul, Soul, you have ample goods laid up for many years; relax, eat, drink, be merry.' But God said to him, 'Fool! This night your soul is required of you, and the things you have prepared, whose will they be?'

Luke 12:16-21

Today could be our last. But Proverbs 21:20 says, "Precious treasure and oil are in a wise man's dwelling, but a foolish man devours it." In other words, a wise man reserves a little for a later day, but the foolish man uses everything up at once. Is the Bible in conflict with itself, here? No. But God does encourage us to strike a balance. It's the difference between saving wisely and hoarding aggressively.

So, by all means, put a plan in place for your later years. The key to it all, though, is to seek God's guidance every step of the way. After all, it's God's money.

Reflection & Mentorship

Begin

- Retirement is not the end; it may be a new beginning for another great stage of life.

Unpack

- Do men think about retirement? If so, when do they start thinking about it, and why?
- When we do think about retirement? Do we have a scriptural view of it or not? Why or why not?

Inform

- Which of the three points and three Scriptures above are the most convicting to you?
- What, in particular, stands out to you in that verse?

Land

- What actionable step do you need to take today?

Do

- Take a step of obedience in how you think and steward this season of your life.

Steps to Giving

If a person gets his attitude toward money straight, it will help straighten out almost every other area in his life.

BILLY GRAHAM

Can we all agree on something? Contributing financially to God's work is not an option. It's commanded as an act of obedience for all followers of Christ. It's not negotiable, even though there are some moments we'd like it to be. And some of us do give in part because God commands us to give. Yet God does not command us to give without providing some guidelines for giving on His terms and in His way. Here are five big guidelines for every man.

Guideline One | Give as you are able.

Every man shall give as he is able, according to the blessing of the Lord your God that He has given you.

Deuteronomy 16:17

It's pretty simple. When God has blessed you abundantly, you give accordingly. When He has blessed you modestly, you give correspondingly. The Old Testament prescribes a tithe, or 10 percent, of your gross income (that's before the income is spent). It's a good rule of thumb.

But the New Testament implies that we should give sacrificially, not just a percentage. So perhaps even when our income is modest, we give abundantly anyway! "Every man shall give as he is able..." leaves us with a lot of latitudes, so yes, it's a matter of heart and prayer. Seek God's guidance and let it be between you and Him.

Guideline Two | Give habitually.

On the first day of every week, each of you is to put something aside and store it up, as he may prosper, so that there will be no collecting when I come.

1 Corinthians 16:2

Giving weekly requires weekly attention. In other words, we need to make it a matter of routine. Let it become part of your regular agenda, to the point where you just do it and not even think about it. A lot of people consider Sunday to be the first day of the week, so that makes it easy if that's when you attend church anyway. Just cast your gift in the offering plate/basket/bag. But maybe you attend a Saturday service or a Wednesday service instead. A lot of churches these days even offer an online option. There are lots of ways to give. The point is, make giving a habit.

Guideline Three | Give to God first.

Honor the Lord with your wealth and with the first fruits of all your produce.

Proverbs 3:9

What are "first fruits"? This means "Budget Item Numero Uno." So put it at the top of the list, ahead of your house payment, your utility bills, and your grocery tab. Make it a priority. Prioritize it like any discipline and be intentional about it.

Guideline Four | Give from joyful motivation.

Each one must give as he has decided in his heart, not reluctantly or under compulsion, for God loves a cheerful giver.

2 Corinthians 9:7

Admittedly, most good habits are formed with an initial decision that may not seem particularly desirable at first. But be encouraged. The joy comes as the practice takes hold. Always be mindful of who you're giving back to and ask Him to work on your heart. God will free you from any lingering reluctance, and your giving eventually will become an act of pure pleasure. Try it–you'll like it!

Guideline Five | Give without expecting something back.

But when you give to the needy, do not let your left hand know what your right hand is doing.

Matthew 6:3

A gift isn't a gift if some kind of return is expected, is it? The real return, of course, is in a lost soul found, a hungry child fed, a homeless family sheltered, or a disciple made. Ultimately, however, the return is God's glory and the building of His kingdom.

So take heart, brothers! Think of what Jesus Christ did for us on the cross. He paid a debt–He did not owe for a debt we could not pay. Kind of puts things in perspective, right? So let us give to the Lord generously–it's the least we can do to show both our willing obedience and love to a generous God who out gives us.

Reflection & Mentorship

Begin

- We are commanded to give to God, but there are a few guidelines.

Unpack

- Do Christian men not give more because they don't know they should or because they don't want to?

Inform

- Of the five Scriptures and points above, which comes easiest for you? Why?
- Of the five Scriptures and points above, which is the most challenging for you? Why?

Land

- What action do you need to take regarding your giving?

Do

- Take one action this week.

Choosing Generosity

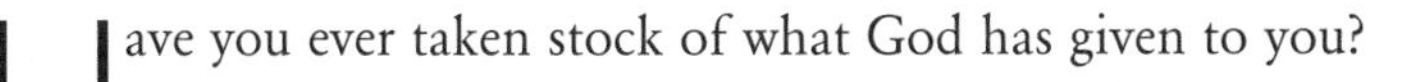

Have you ever taken stock of what God has given to you?

- He died for your sin and the sin of all mankind.
- He redeemed you by buying you back with His Son.
- He provides for your daily needs.
- He promises an eternity in His presence.
- He has adopted you into His family.
- His angels attend to your life.
- He has given your life a purpose and a unique calling.
- His Holy Spirit lives within you daily, providing guidance.

And that is just the tip of the iceberg when you consider the riches of the gifts God provides.

One thing God commands in return is that we give back to Him one-tenth of our income–that's it. The Old Testament calls it a tithe. It's a regular reminder that what we have is not really ours but God's. In stewarding our income this way, we demonstrate that we understand it's really His and not ours. But now consider these facts on tithing from Barna Research:

> *The Barna tracking reported that the proportion of adults who tithed was 7% in 2006 and 2005; 5% in 2004 and 2003; 6% in 2002; and 5% in 2001.*

While God never withholds from us, stats show we regularly hold out on Him. I know it's a challenging statement, and it probably stings a little, but it's true. The facts do not lie.

Keeping it Really, Really, Really Simple

God's economics are not complicated. Take ten one-dollar bills. Put them on the table in front of you where you can see all ten. Take one dollar and put it to the right with a sticky note that says, "For God." Take another dollar and put it to the side with a sticky note that says, "To Save." Then take the other eight and put them in a pile with a sticky note that says, "For Me."

Then repeat the exercise with your monthly income. While the numbers might be larger, the same principle applies, and it's really, really, really simple.

As I said, it is not complicated. But few practice this simple and essential discipline. Even though in the three sticky note piles above, we get 80% of the money we make, we say, "I cannot tithe because I cannot afford it." This is simply not true.

We Make Choices

The church in Corinth was rather affluent. Their people lived like most in the United States do, with more than enough. You've probably got a house, a car, and even a house for your car. Corinth, like our country, was pretty well off too.

But they were lean in their generosity to God.

On his missionary journeys, the apostle Paul collected money for Christians who were under severe persecution and need. But the Corinthian church was holding out by holding on to what they had. While they were wealthier than most, they gave less in percentage than most, as we do today. You can read more about this situation in 2 Corinthians 9.

But instead of ignoring this issue, Paul calls them on the carpet, but not the way you might think. He gives a more positive account of what others had done. In 2 Corinthians 8, Paul tells the Corinthians how generous the Macedonian churches had been. Now, the Macedonian churches were dirt poor. They had almost nothing, but read Paul's description of their response to this need:

We want you to know, brothers, about the grace of God that has been given among the churches of Macedonia, for in a severe test of affliction, their abundance of joy and their extreme poverty have overflowed in a wealth of generosity on their part. For they gave according to their means, as I can testify, and beyond their means, of their own accord, begging us earnestly for the favor of taking part in the relief of the saints–and this, not as we expected, but they gave themselves first to the Lord and then by the will of God to us. Accordingly, we urged Titus that as he had started, so he should complete among you this act of grace. But as you excel in everything–in faith, in speech, in knowledge, in all earnestness, and in our love for you–see that you excel in this act of grace also. - 2 Corinthians 8:1-7).

While the Corinthians were counting their wealth, as it were, and didn't have enough to be generous, the Macedonians were counting their pennies in poverty and still found it possible to be generous.

God's Promise to Those Who Are Generous

Having given the Corinthians the example of the Macedonians, Paul says something profound to them:

> *The point is this: whoever sows sparingly will also reap sparingly, and whoever sows bountifully will also reap bountifully. Each one must give as he has decided in his heart, not reluctantly or under compulsion, for God loves a cheerful giver. And God is able to make all grace abound to you, so that having all sufficiency in all things at all times, you may abound in every good work. As it is written,*
>
> *"He has distributed freely, he has given to the poor;*
> *his righteousness endures forever."*

He who supplies seed to the sower and bread for food will supply and multiply your seed for sowing and increase the harvest of your righteousness. You will be enriched in every way to be generous in every way, which through us will produce thanksgiving to God.

2 Corinthians 9:6-11

If you are not yet tithing, it is worth re-reading these words.

God does not promise that we will become wealthy if we are generous with Him—despite what some promise. But He does say He will bless us in numerous ways, financial or otherwise, and that in all things at all times, having what you need, you will abound in every good work.

That is the life you should want to pursue, and that is the blessing God wants to give, but there is one caveat: Whoever sows sparingly will also reap sparingly, and whoever sows generously will also reap bountifully. Do you want to reap sparingly or generously? That is the choice each of us makes.

Reflection & Mentorship

Begin

- Tithing, or giving 10 percent to God, is required of all followers of Christ. It's a response to God's generosity.

Unpack

- How does the fact that few Christians practice the tithe strike you?
- Why is this so? Do we have a wrong understanding of money, or is it a concern about something else?

Inform

- What insights do you gain from 2 Corinthians 9:6-11?
- What does "He distributed freely" mean?
- Why does Paul say the following? "He who supplies seed to the sower and bread for food will supply and multiply your seed for sowing and increase the harvest of your righteousness. You will be enriched in every way to be generous in every way, which through us will produce thanksgiving to God."

Land

- What needs to change regarding your practice of tithing?

Do

- What action do you need to take today?

Save for Emergencies

Go to the ant, O sluggard; consider her ways, and be wise. Without having any chief, officer, or ruler, she prepares her bread in summer and gathers her food in harvest.

PROVERBS 6:6-8

What happens when you have an emergency that taps the finances? Let's say the transmission goes out on your car, or the condenser dies on the refrigerator, or your roof, and you have a lot of it, needs repair? For most, the answer is immediately to put it on that high-interest credit card and get the issue resolved. And after only a few emergencies, that credit card ends up carrying a large balance (as it may have been even before the crisis), and we discover one day we are in financial bondage.

How much better it would be if you had the money to meet the typical emergency need without going into debt to do so. There is a sense of freedom in paying cash for that rebuilt transmission and know that it is done. Putting it on your card is merely delaying the full payment and penalizing yourself in the process. In the end, you end up paying for that transmission twice or more by the time it is paid off.

There is another caveat to this issue. Men are called to provide, yet every time we incur debt (especially consumer debt), we are reducing our ability to provide for our family. Yes, we may meet the immediate need, but we are greatly diminishing our ability to meet other needs.

What message does this communicate to others when we must meet predictable emergencies with growing credit debt? This becomes a sinkhole for many men called to provide and to be wise about how to do it. The inadvertent message is, "I am not disciplined enough to save for predictable emergencies." I don't know about you, but that is not the message I want to communicate to my spouse or family, or even my extended family.

The book of Proverbs is amazingly practical, and Proverbs 6:6-8 above puts this into perspective. The "sluggard" is a lazy individual who does not save up for a day of emergency or expected need. No one wants to be called a "sluggard," but let's be honest–saving is a matter of discipline, and sluggards are not disciplined. This wisdom saying suggests that even tiny insects know how to store up their food, so they have enough when food isn't readily available.

Prior generations lived by different rules than us. They saved enough to care for their family in times of need. After all, they didn't have a credit card to fall back on. Easy credit has made Americans lazy when it comes to money–we all know this is true. Even filing for bankruptcy is welcomed and acceptable for those who have made a series of bad financial decisions. It has lured us into thinking we can finance our lives on credit, and it's easy to do. Over a lifetime, this can cost us an enormous sum, cause us to be lazy with one of the most critical aspects of our lives, and cause us to live in financial bondage rather than economic freedom.

There is a better way–developing the discipline to save a portion of each month's income so we have reserves for the day we need them. A basic rule of thumb is to give God 10 percent off the top of every paycheck, as God teaches. Next, we tithe to ourselves 10 percent for savings. We then have 80 percent of our income to use as we choose.

This principle keeps our resources in perspective. God owns our resources, so we honor him by returning to him the "first fruits" of our work. Then we acknowledge ourselves and our families by putting 10 percent into savings to provide for needs in the future. In doing this, we honor God, ourselves, and our families.

This is about is developing financial freedom rather than living in financial bondage. Financial bondage is consumer debt. Not only making payments monthly but paying the interest on borrowed funds and watching our disposable income shrink because of our fees, which usually mount over time because we are not being disciplined to save.

It's a matter of discipline, which is why Proverbs calls the undisciplined individual away from sluggardly living. It's the discipline to live within our means, to save for a rainy day and to limit our expenditures so that we avoid consumer debt and can put money away for emergencies and the future.

There is nothing men desire more than respect. Financial discipline enables us to respect ourselves, and it gains the respect of others who see that we are committed to providing for them with our funds rather than borrowed funds. Anyone can be a sluggard, but it takes discipline to be a saver. Go to the ant.

Start with your next paycheck. Please don't wait until you can afford it. You cannot afford not to do it. Start now! Be like the ant, not the sluggard.

Reflection & Mentorship

Begin

- The disciplined man saves for emergencies.

Unpack

- Do you know men who save? How do they do it?
- Are you a saver or a spender? Be honest.

Inform

Go to the ant, O sluggard; consider her ways, and be wise. Without having any chief, officer, or ruler, she prepares her bread in summer and gathers her food in harvest.

Proverbs 6:6-8

- When you read the Scripture, what stands out to you?
- How systematic and disciplined is the ant?
- In contrast, how do you think the "sluggard" acts?

Land

- What do you need to do to be more disciplined in this area?

Do

- What is one step you can take today?
- Confess this to someone you trust.

Kingdom Investments

Sell your possessions, and give to the needy. Provide yourselves with moneybags that do not grow old, with a treasure in the heavens that does not fail, where no thief approaches and no moth destroys.

LUKE 12:33

For where your treasure is, there your heart will be also.

MATTHEW 6:21

One of the most robust investment strategies we can make in life is kingdom investments–investing in God's work while living our natural life. Consider this: Some things cross the line from time into eternity. One of these things is the lives we have touched because we invested in God's work. Everything else stays, but not our eternal investments. They go with us.

The financial investments we make regularly will come and go in value, but the investments we make in ministry never fail, and nothing can stop the amount they accrue. You cannot take your wealth with you at your death, but you can send it ahead of you through generous kingdom investments. Every time you give generously to God's work, you are sending your treasures ahead of you, and one day in heaven, you will personally meet those whose lives were touched by the investments you made.

There is another principle at work here as well. Jesus also states, "For where your treasure is, there your heart will be also." If our goal is to accumulate toys and wealth, our hearts will be captivated by our stuff and the limited reach of the security that this stuff provides–which is not much. Also, our hearts are directly impacted by what we spend our money on. If our goal is to hold on to it, our hearts will be invested in retention and protection. If our goal is to spend it on the things of this life, then our hearts will be invested in the objects of interest. If our goal is to give as much as we can to God's work, our hearts will be invested in Jesus' intent and mission. It is that simple.

And like all other investments, kingdom investments require a strategy. Most people start with a tithe, but some take it a step further. These people find ways to invest all of God's money in things of eternal value and seek to see their continual investment. This begins by admitting that money can command and grip our hearts and gradually loosening the grip it has on us. Money has a seductive power that can quickly grab our hearts and focus our lives on the wrong things. As we learn to direct and steward our money, we are also learning to lead and guide our hearts.

Giving to God and his work opens the door for us to greater generosity to God because when we are aligned with God's mission, we are no longer captivated and seduced by money. Paul puts generosity in perspective when he writes to the Corinthians:

The point is this: whoever sows sparingly will also reap sparingly, and whoever sows bountifully will also reap bountifully. Each one must give as he has decided in his heart, not reluctantly or under compulsion, for God loves a cheerful giver. And God is able to make all grace abound to you, so that having all sufficiency in all things at all times, you may abound in every good work. - 2 Corinthians 9:6-8

So what are the benefits of generosity to God and His work–in making kingdom investments?

First, when we invest in the kingdom, we are storing up treasures in an eternal account. Given a choice between an account at your local bank or God's bank, it seems a no-brainer to choose God's bank because the investment is assured with significant backing.

Second, when we invest in the kingdom, we are impacting lives for eternity. Our goal is to make heaven more crowded and hell less crowded. That is why Jesus came. I love to imagine one day when I get to heaven someone tapping me on the shoulder and thanking me for playing a part in bringing them to Christ. I might even turn and say, "Do I know you?" Then they answer, "No, but your investment made it possible. So thank you." Only in eternity will we discover much of this, but our generosity here makes the difference.

Third, when we invest in the kingdom, we make the world a better place. Jesus taught us to pray, "Thy will be done on earth as it is in heaven." He desires to see poverty eased, people in need served, righteous laws upheld, the marginalized cared for, physical needs met, and the list could go on. When our kingdom investments bring both the gospel of Jesus and the values of Jesus to our world, the world becomes a better place. We get to invest in this during our lifetime.

Fourth, when we invest in the kingdom, the grip of materialism, money, and wealth is broken. Money is not bad, as some say, but the grip of money on our hearts is deadly. The more generous we are with God, the less of a grip our stuff has on us. We recognize that we are stewards and not owners and that we can invest in things that count for eternity.

All of us have investments. Let's have the courage to make kingdom investments as essential as our other investments. You cannot take it with you, but you can send it ahead of you.

Reflection & Mentorship

Begin

- There are all kinds of investments we can make, but kingdom investments make an eternal impact.

Unpack

- Have you ever thought about your kingdom investment?
- How does one make kingdom investments during his lifetime?

Inform

For where your treasure is, there your heart will be also.

Matthew 6:21

- What do treasures tell us about the heart?
- What do our hearts tell us about our treasures?

Land

- How is your heart concerned about the things of God?
- What changes need to be addressed?

Do

- Make one kingdom investment today.

Wise Counsel

Without counsel, plans fail, but with many advisers they succeed.

PROVERBS 15:22

Blessed is the man who walks not in the counsel of the wicked, nor stands in the way of sinners, nor sits in the seat of scoffers.

PSALMS 1:1

Precious treasure and oil are in a wise man's dwelling, but a foolish man devours it.

PROVERBS 21:20

There are certain areas of a man's life where the counsel of others is critical, but where we find it hard to ask for help. One of these is money.

But why are men hesitant to ask for help in the area of money and finances?

I think there are several reasons:

- Shame: We know that we have messed up with our finances—living on the financial edge, debt, purchases that we could not afford. Men don't like to reveal their weaknesses to other men, and our shame often keeps us from getting help.
- Self-Reliance: We think we ought to be able to figure money out ourselves. The truth is that many of us were not taught how to handle finances, and many lack the necessary skills to manage them well. Our belief that we should be self-reliant hurts us more as each month goes by, and we continue unhealthy practices.
- Self-love: I don't want others to know that I don't know how to handle money properly and that I need help. My pride keeps me from looking for help even though I need it.

How do we handle these personal issues that keep us from getting the help we need? We humble ourselves to seek counsel. Proverbs 15:22 says it all above. The mark of a godly man is humility, not pride. Humility is being willing to admit mistakes, failures, or a need to learn. Why? So we can be the men God designed us to be and not live in fear, shame, or ignorance.

Where Do We Find Help for Our Financial Questions?

It is essential to develop a biblical understanding of money, finances, budgeting, debt, and sound financial decision-making. One way to do this is to seek out other men who have done an excellent job with their finances and have had success biblically. Ask them to share with you what they know and how they handle their finances. Consider gathering a group of men who want to openly discuss the topic of finances and learn with one another and encourage one another.

Ground rules for such a group include:

- Sharing candidly about the issues you are facing
- Being confidential with what you have heard from others

- Attending with an attitude of humility rather than pride
- Praying for one another
- Celebrating the successes of one another

There are also those from who we should not take counsel. Psalm 1:1 says, "Blessed is the man who walks not in the counsel of the wicked, nor stands in the way of sinners, nor sits in the seat of scoffers." Be aware that some financial advice is the counsel of the ungodly–advertising that declares we will be happy if we purchase the next toy. Those who sell credit, whether credit cards or home equity loans, which promise that they are the answer to your financial needs while taking you further into financial bondage. Or salespeople who tell you that your purchase is an excellent investment.

Before one makes a significant purchase or accepts the counsel of those who are selling products, it is an excellent policy to consult outside friends and advisors and remember what you have learned in your study of biblical financial principles. If in doubt, then don't do it. If pressured for a quick decision, then walk away. If you have not prayed about it, then wait.

One principle that too few of us follow in this day of easy credit it that of saving. Proverbs 21:20 says this: "Precious treasure and oil are in a wise man's dwelling, but a foolish man devours it." Having treasures in our possession (savings) rather than spending what we have regularly is one of the most basic of financial disciplines. Savings give us options while spending what we have does not. The lack of budgeting, savings, and financial discipline is at the core of most financial difficulties.

Don't let shame, self-reliance, or pride keep you from discovering the fantastic gift of financial freedom. We have all paid dumb tax with finances. Don't pay more. Get counsel, teaching, and advice for a new perspective on money.

Reflection & Mentorship

Begin

- If we don't have wise counsel, we should ask for the sake of our finances.

Unpack

- Do you have a counselor you can talk with about your finances (professional or otherwise)? Why or why not?
- How have they helped you in the past?

Inform

- Of the three texts above, which one commands your attention the most? And why?

Land

- What kind of counsel do you need right now when it comes to your finances?
- What steps do you need to take today?

Do

- Build a friendship with a Christian man who is financially wise.

20 Lessons That Build a Man's Faith:

A Conversational Mentoring Guide

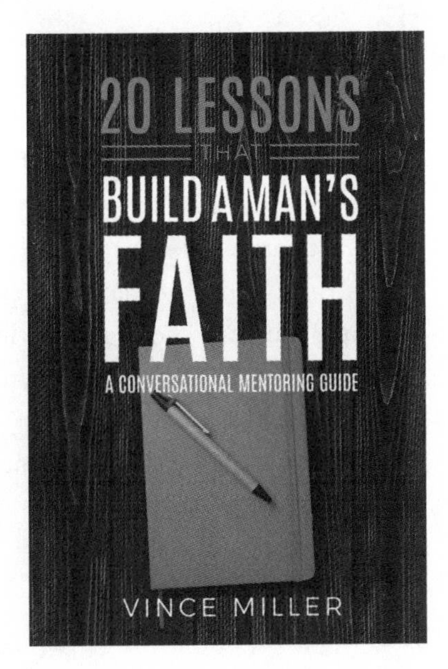

Every man has a crystallizing moment in his faith–the moment he decides to surrender his life completely to Christ. From that instant, life is never the same; he is a new creation. However, there are some men who struggle with where to begin in their walk with the Lord. They just aren't sure where to start in order to grow their faith, and they lack the support of fellow Christians in community or one-on-one mentorship.

In 20 Lessons That Build a Man's Faith, author Vince Miller guides and teaches men how to walk with Christ using fundamental spiritual practices including: reading the Bible, solitude, journaling, and quiet times.

$12.99 paperback

128 pages

ISBN: 978-1-946453-95-2

https://beresolute.org/product/20-lessons-that-build-a-mans-faith/

20 Lessons That Build a Man's Family:

A Conversational Mentoring Guide

Being the husband, father, and leader your family needs is one of the great challenges you'll face as a man. It will test you to the core. And it will make you, or it will break you–daily. But these roles are your greatest leadership opportunity and they have the power to shape you into the man and leader God created you to be. Engage in life-changing discussions with other men to grow in your character as a man in community with others!

$10.99 paperback

112 pages

ISBN: 978-1-946453-81-5

https://beresolute.org/product/20-lessons-that-build-a-mans-family/